THE AUTHOR'S GUIDE...

Lawrence Okon

The Author's Guide

Copyright © January 2019 Lawrence Okon
All rights reserved. No part of this publication may be
reproduced, distributed, or transmitted in any form or by

any means, including photocopying, recording, or other electronic or mechanical methods, without the prior written permission of the publisher, except in the case of brief quotations embodied in critical reviews and certain other noncommercial uses permitted by copyright law. For more information, contact: readempire.com

DISCLAIMER

This book and the contents provided herein are simply for education, general Information purposes only. They do not (and should not) take the place of legal advice from your lawyer. It is sold with the understanding that the publisher is not engaged in rendering legal, accountingor other professional service. Every effort has been made to ensure that the content provided in this book isaccurate and helpful for our readers at publishing time. However, this is not an exhaustive treatment of the subjects. The author has made every effort to ensure the accuracy of the

CONTENTS

Chapter 1

Chapter 2

Lesson15: Write a compelling opener that keeps your reader in a state of wow.

Lesson 16: Your story should be filled with conflict and tension.

Lesson 17: Concentrate on writing a first draft, don't worry about editing.

Lesson 18: Stay put till you are done.

Lesson19: Give a remarkable ending.

Lesson 20: Get a mentor.

Chapter 3

Lesson 21: Your expectations.

Lesson 22: How to get your books published faster.

Lesson 23: Your books are rejected? This is what you need to do.

Lesson 24: Why your books might never get published.

Lesson 25: You have been offered a contract, don't rush.

Lesson 26: Why your book represent a risk to your publisher.

Lesson 27: what is good for you as an unknown author is a moderate advance.

Lesson 28: Why you don't want a tiny advance either.

Lesson 29: The wise editor and the fool writer.

Lesson 30: Printing your books.

Chapter 4

Chapter 5

Chapter 6

Lesson 51: Is that all I get?

Lesson 52: The Writing business?

Lesson 53: Changing publishers.

Lesson 54: Dealing with Foreign and Local Taxes

Lesson 55: Anyone who can be discouraged from writing should be.

INTRODUCTION

The writing journey can be so diffficult to walk alone, that's why I'm here to walk alongside with you and empower you on your journey and get you to where you believe you can be.

There are some secret you should never trade for anything, like the advice I got from those who walked the path before me and I never take it for granted. So why pay the price of failing before succeeding when you can follow someone that has been there and copy from them, the simplest way to becoming successful in this path you have chosen is to copy and apply the same principle legends that have walked the path you are walking on right now have chosen.

That's the reason this book is here to serve you in the best possible way it can. I see too many amateur writers make easily avoidable mistakes that keep

them from advancing in their careers. Mistakes I call the harmless circle but in itself very dangerous.

I want help make sure you don't do the same if you will allow me and that's exactly why this book is in your hands because you have chosen to succeed in this field you have chosen. The goal is to get your writing up to where you could ever want it to be. The simple truth is if you'll stay focused and apply what I will teach you, you're going to be amazed at your progress over the next couple of weeks if you put all I'm going to teach you into practice: And few things are guarantee

❖   *You'll avoid the mistakes that keep people from taking your writing seriously even if you haven't written any piece before this great piece of Gold in a book is for you.*

❖   *You'll learn to deeply move your reader and get them begging you for more.*

❖   *You'll multiply your chances of getting published especially if you're writing a book.*

I'll reveal writing secrets my mentors and the big authors in the industry shared with me even those I've never shared before, as well as fundamentals I emphasize over and over because they're so important for every writer to know am so glad our path came across. Let the fun begin.

❖ ❖ ❖

Since You Decided To Be an Author.

Being an author has change a lot of peoples life, even my my life not to mention the opportunity given to you to impact thousands, even millions, of people that you will never get to met in your entire lifetime.
However as an author for these few years, I can tell you: It's far easier to quit than to finish. When you run out of ideas, when your own message bores you, or when you become overwhelmed by the scope of the task of completing that piece of idea that is in you, you're going to be tempted to give up; I want to tell you the absolute truth.

But here is something that can make a huge difference:

If you know where to start from in this journey of writing
If you know what each step entails in this journey.
If you know how to overcome fear, procrastination, and   writer's block even in your worst precarious state you will be so glad you choose this part.
If you know how to keep from feeling overwhelmed and stressed out etc

If you have all these in place believe me you *can* do this and more quickly than you might think, because these days and age writers have access to more writing tools than ever. The key is to follow a proven, straightforward, step by-step plan and below I outline some that I thought are really relevant and will be useful to you.

CHAPTER 1

*Lesson1: Can anyone venture
into writing?*

I know you have met people that brag about writing? I mean people that make writing looks so easy but yet they haven't written up to 50 page of any inspiring content. Writers often meet people who assume that writing is easy. You will meet them, in your offices, in your school, in recreational centre etc "I'm going to write a book one day when I get the time," or "I'm going to take six months off and write a book and then I'll use the advance to write full time, pay off the mortgage, acquire this, get that, get this done and so forth."

Writing isn't easy and, even after you've been doing it for a few years, you're still a novice in the business of writing, it is a skill that constantly requires rebranding and reinventing of self, you don't what to be the guy that your readers after reading two of your literary piece would predict what you will do next, that will be a lash on your back and you don't expect such individual to want to read your piece again and having no readers equals to having no sells and absolutely no one to read your big idea. So if you want to be a successful writer, be prepared to work as hard, and as long, as if you wanted to be a violinist in an orchestra, a professional cricketer or a doctor. Rarely, someone will write a book and get it published straight away, but that's pretty un-usual unless your father owns a publishing house and has maybe enough money to through away in exception of self publishing all thanks to technology and platform like Amazon kindle pub-lishing. I was once in a roomful of writers when that question was asked, and only three writers raised their hands. Most writers work for 5-10 years before getting their first book published.

Remember the 10,000-hour rule. That's roughly how much work

and practice it takes to become accomplished in any field, whether you are into sporting, creative or professional field. 10,000 hours is 5 years of full time hard work. To become a virtuoso, isn't that crazy but to become a best seller in the writing industry triple that,

you have to be obese with your ideas not only that you got to find away to convince people that you got a story to tell, how do you do that apart from giving them a proof in with your literary work.

Let me tell you a secret to the success of one guy I love in the music industry.

This guy in an interview narrated how all he does is music to the extent that if a plate fails on the ground he finds meaning to the sound that plate makes, if he sleeps he is thinking about his music, if he is walking, bathing, jogging, whatever happened around him, he had a way of connecting it to his music, you can see the level of commitment he puts into his craft how much more a writer that invites people into his or her realm of intellectual sensuality.

Lesson 2: The need for a writing place

To write your book, you don't need the most comfortable place in the world or in your home, you just need a space away from distraction, where you can connect and reason with the reality of the moment. All you need to do is to dedicate a room or a particular section in your home, office or wherever you are for these task because the nicer and more comfortable and private you can make your writing space the better.

Real writers can write anywhere. Some write in restaurants and coffee shops. I write in my bedroom, sometimes in my library all you need to write is just to find what works for you.

◆ ◆ ◆

Lesson 3: Get all you need
for writing together

I have always written my work using my laptop. Most author do, though some handwrite their first drafts and then keyboard them onto a computer or pay someone to do that depending on the time at their disposal or their financial capacity.

No publisher would even consider a manuscript submitted in handwriting.
The publishing industry runs on Microsoft Word, so you'll need to submit Word document files. Whether you prefer a Mac or a PC, both will produce the kinds of files you need.

What else do you need? If you are one who handwrites your first drafts, don't scrimp on paper, pencils, or erasers.
Don't shortchange yourself on a computer either. Even if someone else typing the word as you speaks, you'll need your computer for research and for communicating with potential agents, editors, publishers.

Get the best computer you can afford, the latest, the one with the most capacity and speed and the one you are comfortable with.

Try to imagine *everything* you're going to need in addition to your desk or table, so you can equip yourself in advance and don't have to keep interrupting your work to find things like stapler, paper clips, a ruler, a pencil holder, a sharpener, note pads, printing paper, paperweights, a tape dispenser, cork or bulletin board the list goes on.

Last, get the best, most comfortable chair.
Get a straight-backed chair or something similar and be proactive about your posture and maintain a healthy spine.
There's nothing worse than trying to be creative and immerse yourself in writing while you're in serious pains cause by a bad posture.
Get a comfortable chair it mustn't cost you thousands of dollars before it will be comfortable.

If you've never used some of the items I listed above and can't imagine needing them, fine. But make a list of

everything you *know* you'll need so when the actual writing begins, you're already equipped for the job.

Lesson 4: Begin by break your writing plans down

Writing a book feels like a colossal project, maybe because it is! But you have to remember your manuscript will be made up of many small parts. I want you to remember that saying a journey of a thousand miles begins with a step right? Apply it when writing your books.

Try to get your mind off your book as a 600-or-so-page monstrosity. It can't be written all at once any more than like climbing a ladder to a rooftop.

See your book for what it is: a manuscript made up of sentences, paragraphs, pages although it might look like it never going to be what you project in your head. But you got to know that those pages will begin to add up, and though after a week you may have barely accumulated double digits, a few months down the road you'll be into your second hundred pages.

So keep it simple start by distilling your big book idea from a page or so to a single sentence—your premise. The more specific that one-sentence premise, the more it will keep you focused while you're writing.

Wait let's not run faster than ourselves, before you can turn your big idea into one sentence, which can then be expanded to an outline, you have to settle on exactly what that big idea is or is going to be.

Lesson 5: Focus on your big idea?

To be book-worthy, your idea has to be killer. You need to write something about which you're passionate, something that gets you up in the morning, draws you to the keyboard, and keeps you there. It should excite not only you, but also anyone you tell about it. I can't overstate the importance of this. If you've

tried and failed to finish your book before—maybe more than once or twice it could be that the basic premise was flawed, maybe your so called big idea couldn't carry an entire book and most importantly it should align with what the public will resonate with unless you are just writing for the passion and gratification that comes with being an author and not really for the money.

Think, *Harry Potter*, The market is crowded, the competition fierce. There's no more room for run of-the-mill ideas. Your premise alone should make readers salivate, long for more of your brain power and that's how you can stay on top of your game.

How do you know you've got a winning book at the first place? If it does gives you reason to sacrifice all for it, I mean does it stay in your mind, growing and developing every time you think of it? Run it past loved ones, friends and others you trust. Does it raise eyebrows? Elicit Wows? Or does it result in awkward silences?

The right idea simply works, and you'll know it when you land on it, it it's like finish a hidden talent. Most importantly, your idea must capture *you* in such a way that you're compelled to write it, it should be able to keep you awake all night thinking about how your audience are going to be shocked. Otherwise you'll lose interest halfway through and never finish that's the whole truth.

◆ ◆ ◆

Lesson 6: Put your outline into perspectives

Starting your writing without a clear vision of where you're going will usually end in disaster. Any project without a specific plan and strategy to achieve it will end in a messy way.

you should always put interesting characters in difficult situations and write to find out what happens.

Learn to fashion some sort of a directional document that provides structure and also serves as a safety net. If you get out on that pro level that you thought you were and lose your balance, you'll thank me for advising you to have this in place.

If you're writing a nonfiction book, there's no substitute for an outline that is usually what will keep you on the big idea. Potential agents or publishers require this in your proposal. They want to know where you're going, and they want to know that you know. What do you want your reader to learn from your book, and how will you ensure they learn it? Fiction or nonfiction, if you commonly lose interest in your book somewhere in your journey to write that big story it's you didn't start with enough exciting ideas. That's why and outline (or a basic framework) is essential.

Don't even start writing until you're confident your structure will hold up through the end.

You may recognize this novel structure illustration. Did you know it holds up—with only slight adaptations—for nonfiction books too? It's self-explanatory for novelists; they list their plot twists and developments and arrange them in an order that best serves to increase tension.

What separates great nonfiction from mediocre? The same structure! Arrange your points and evidence in the same way so you're setting your reader up for a huge payoff, and then make sure you deliver on your promise of getting their emotions so intense in what you have promise.

If your nonfiction book is a memoir, an autobiography, or a biography, structure it like a novel and you can't go wrong.

But even if it's a straightforward how-to get out of anxiety, stay as close to this structure as possible, and you'll see your manuscript come alive. Make promises early, triggering your reader to anticipate fresh ideas, secrets, inside information, something major that will make him thrilled with the finished product.

While you may not have as much action or dialogue or character development as your novelist counterpart, your crises and tension can come from showing where people have failed before and how you're going to ensure your reader will succeed. You can even make the how-to project look impossible until you pay off that setup with your unique solution.
Keep your outline to a single page. But make sure every major point is represented, so you'll always know where you're going.
And don't worry if you've forgotten the basics of classic outlining or have never felt comfortable with the concept. Your outline must serve you. If that means Roman numerals and capital and lowercase letters and then Arabic numerals, you can certainly fashion it that way. But if you just want a list of sentences that synopsize your idea, that's fine too it just what will keep you on track.

Simply start with your working title, then your premise, then—for fiction, list all the major scenes that fit into the rough structure above. For nonfiction, try to come up with chapter titles and a sentence or two of what each chapter will cover or a sticky note that reminds you of what that chapter entails.

Once you have your one-page outline, remember it is a just a document meant to serve you and your book. Expand it, change it, play with it as you see fit—even during the writing process when you land on a bigger or better scene for the next chapter.

◆ ◆ ◆

Lesson 7: Stick to your writing schedule

Normally, you would want to write whenever you feel like you have the inspiration or motivation to do so but I would advise you schedule at least six hours per week to write. That may consist of three sessions of two hours each, two sessions of three hours, or six one-hour sessions—whatever works for you is okay. A regular pattern (same times, same days) that can most easily become a habit and it will give you the success you want and remember whatever you do for at least 21 days nonstop has the capacity to become a habit. But if that's impossible, just make sure you carve out at least six hours so you can see real progress.

Having trouble finding the time to write a book? Having so much distractions that you are bother it can't work for you? You have to *make* it work. You just have to create that time. That's what it takes. Something in your calendar will likely have to be sacrificed in the interest of writing time. Make sure it's not your family—they should always be your top priority. Never sacrifice your family on the altar of your writing career because you will end up having regrets, imagine you are a mum that has a baby that looks up to you for everything it will be unwise not to give that child the required attention that you should.

But beyond that, the truth is that we all find time for what we really want to do.
Many writers insist they have no time to write, but they always seem to catch the latest Netflix original series, or go to the next big Hollywood or Nollywood movies. They enjoy concerts, parties, football etc.

How important is it to you to finally write your book? What will you cut from your calendar each week to *ensure* you give it the time it deserves?

- A game?
- A party?
- Less of chatting or scrolling through social media?
- A favorite TV show?
- An hour of sleep per night? (You have to be careful with this one because rest is crucial to a writer.)

To become a successful writer you have to make time to write and every successful writer does exactly that.
When writing becomes a habit, you'll be on your way to fulfilling that dream of becoming an author and I know you will.

❖ ❖ ❖

Lesson 8: Set a Reasonable Deadline

Most people hardly or rarely get anything done without deadlines. A deadline does give you that motivation you need to complete any task including your book. Some of you your deadlines will be established in your contracts from the publishers. If you're writing your first book, you probably don't have a contract yet. To ensure you finish your book, set your own deadline—then consider it sacred. Tell your spouse or loved one or trusted friend. Ask that they hold you accountable, or you could bet with then with some little amount of penny and tell them if you don't finish up before the deadline they are entitle to that money, the idea is that someone should hold you accountable.

Now determine—and enter in your calendar—the number of pages you need to produce per writing session to meet your deadline. If it proves unrealistic, change the deadline now. If you have no idea how many pages or words you typically produce per session, you may have to experiment before you finalize those figures. Say you want to finish a 400-page manuscript by this time next year. Divide 400 by 50 weeks (accounting for two off-weeks), and you get eight pages per week.

Divide that by your typical number of writing sessions per week and you'll know how many pages you should finish per session. Now is the time to adjust these numbers, while setting your deadline and determining your pages per session. Maybe you'd rather schedule four off weeks over the next year. Or you know your book will be unusually long. Change the numbers to make it realistic and doable, and then lock it in. Remember, your deadline is sacred journal and it shouldn't and mustn't be abused.

Lesson 9: Welcome procras-tination (sometimes)

I know we were taught that procrastination is the lazy man excuse, but I want to tell you this about procrastination. Don't fight it; embrace it, that's the goodness you can do for yourself procrastinate a lot and if you are surprise you shouldn't be. So many authors are procrastinators that I've come to wonder if it's a prerequisite.

The secret is to accept it and, in fact, *schedule* it.

I quit fretting and losing sleep over procrastinating when I realized it was inevitable and predictable, and also that it was productive. So you might want to ask how does procrastination helps me. I believe you have heard the saying that if you don't create a day to rest, your body will chose a day you won't like and you won't have any say or anything to do about it. Sound like rationalization? Maybe it was at first. But I learned that while I'm putting off the writing, my subconscious is working on my book. It's a part of the process; it also allows you to be open to wilder imagination.

When you *do* start writing again, you'll enjoy the surprises your subconscious reveals to you during that period of procrastinating. So, knowing procrastination is coming, book it on your calendar. Take it into account when you're determining your page quotas. If you have to go back in and increase the number of pages you need to produce per session, do that.

And here's the key—you must never let things get to where that number of pages per day exceeds your capacity if you do then you are in for worry and anxiety. It's one thing to ratchet up your output from two pages per session to three. But if you let it get out of hand, you've violated the sacredness of your deadline which you shouldn't have abused.

◆ ◆ ◆

*Lesson 10: Kill all distractions
and stay focus*

Have you found yourself writing a sentence and then checking your email? Writing another and checking Facebook? Or feel like checking up on your boo or getting hocked up in a new comedy show on YouTube? Like seriously are you as easily distracted as I am?

One distraction that leads to more and more, once you are in your writing is forgotten, and all of a sudden the day has gotten away from you and you are far behind schedule.

If your case is like mine you need to take a look at this applications that help deal with insidious timewasters? these apps allows you to block your email, social media, browsers, game apps, whatever you wish during the hours you want to write. Some carry a little fee, others are free you can try them out and stick with the one that works for you.

1. Stay Focused
2. Focus Writer
3. Freedom App
4. WriteRoom etc

Use them to keep curtain your procrastination and be more productive in your writing career.

CHAPTER 2

Lesson 11: Do your research

One thing you should know about research is that research is a vital part of the process and successful writers know this, whether you're writing fiction or nonfiction. Fiction means more than just making up a story. Your details and logic and technical and historical details must be right for your novel to be believable and acceptable.

And for nonfiction, even if you're writing about a subject in which you're an expert like the does and don't of gentlemen you'll be surprised how ensuring you gets all the facts right will polish your finished product. In fact, you'd be surprised at how many times I've researched a fact or two while writing this book

The last thing you want is even a small mistake due to your lack of proper research. Regardless the detail, trust me, you'll hear from readers about it.

Your credibility as an author and an expert hinges on creating trust with your reader. That dissolves in a hurry if you commit an error whether it was intentional or not it's none of their business and they won't excuse you for any excuse you provide.

Here are some famous favorite research resources that most writers use:

World Almanacs: These alone list almost everything you need for accurate prose: facts, data, government information, and more about your subject of interest.

The Merriam-Webster Thesaurus: The online version is a great tool for search of words, because it's really fast. You couldn't turn the pages of a hard copy as quickly as you can get where you want to onscreen. One caution: Never let it be obvious you've consulted a thesaurus. You're not looking for the exotic word that jumps off the page. You're looking for that common word that's on the tip of your tongue which can trill your readers and at the same times leave them impressed.

WorldAtlas.com: This one is a great tool in your writing,you'll find nearly limitless information about any continent, country, region, city, town, or village. Names, monetary units, weather patterns, tourism info, and even facts you wouldn't have thought of.

Lesson 12: Start calling yourself a writer

Your friends might think you are crazy by calling yourself a writer and having nothing to show for it, I remember when I first published my first book and come to think about it, it was on relationship I got mixed feelings about it because it was a subject considered not fit for everyone to get involve with.

You see the thing is your inner voice may tell you, "You're no writer and you never will be. What do you think you're doing, trying to write a book?

That may be why you've stalled at writing your book in the past. But if you're working at writing, studying writing, practicing writing, that makes you a writer. Don't wait till you reach some artificial level of accomplishment before calling yourself a writer. A carpenter is a carpenter whether he's ever built a house or not same WERwith a teacher whether he has ever step his foot in the classroom or not.

Self-identify as a writer now and you'll silence that inner critic—who, of course, is really you. Talk back to yourself if you must it may sound silly, but acknowledging yourself as a writer can give you the confidence to keep going and finish your book. So if you indeed want to be a writer start calling yourself one.

Lesson 13: The book is not about you, think reader-first

Must time people ask me how can I write a best seller, well this is the only way, you have to realize that readers first is so important that you should write it on a sticky note and affix it to your monitor so you're reminded of it every time you write or place it where your eyes will always come across it, when you lift your head in your writing time.

Every decision you make about your manuscript must be run through this filter, the reader-first, not you-first, not book-first, not editor-, agent-, or publisher-first.

Certainly not your inner circle- or critics-first, reader-first, last, and always that's how you get a bestseller.

If every decision is based on the idea of reader-first, when fans tells you they were moved by one of your books you will get to understand more.

Does a scene bore you? If you're thinking reader-first, it gets overhauled or deleted without any further consideration.

Where to go, what to say, what to write next? Decide based on the reader as your priority.

Whatever your gut tells you your reader would prefer, that's your answer don't try to argue with it. If it suggests you should get rid of a character you have too, Why? The reason is simple, if you are not feeling a particular character as a writer how much more your readers who expect nothing else from you but the best.

Whatever will intrigue him, move him, keep him reading, those are your marching orders. So, naturally, you need to know your reader much really well, you should know their rough age, General interests, their love, what they hate, your readers attention span? Etc

The surest way to please your reader is to please yourself. Write what you would want to read and trust there is a broad readership out there that agrees, be your own critic, narrate a particular character to your kids, friends and observe their reactions that's how you win.

◆ ◆ ◆

Lesson14: Find your writing voice

Discovering your voice is not as complicated as some make it to be. Your writing voice is just the unique way you relate a particular incident to another person and no one else can do it better that you. You can find yours by answering these quick questions:

1. What's the coolest thing that ever happened to you?
2. who's the most important person you told about it?
3. What did you sound like when you did?

That's your writing voice. It should read the way you sound at your most engaged. Write it the same way you would have narrated the story, that's all there is to it.

If you write fiction and the narrator of your book isn't you, go through the three-question exercise on the narrator's behalf—and you'll quickly master the voice

◆ ◆ ◆

Lesson15: Write a compelling opener that keeps your reader in a state of wow

This is where it all begins, and a lot of writers suck when it comes to this, if you're stuck because of the pressure of crafting the perfect opening line, well you need not worry. This is not something you should put off and come back to once you've started on the rest of the first chapter. Although, it can still change if the story dictates that, but settling on a good one will really get you off and running. It's unlikely you'll write a more important sentence than your first one, whether you're writing fiction or nonfiction.

Make sure you're thrilled with it and then watch how your confidence and momentum soars and give yourself the credits you deserve when it is requires.

Most great first lines fall into one of these categories I found from other great writers I believe you must have come across them before:

1. Surprising

Fiction: "It was a bright cold day in April, and the clocks were striking thirteen."
—George Orwell, *Nineteen Eighty-Four*
Nonfiction: "By the time Eustace Conway was seven years old, he could throw a knife accurately enough to nail a chipmunk to a tree." —Elizabeth Gilbert, *The Last American Man*

2. Dramatic Statement

Fiction: "They shoot the white girl first." —Toni Morrison, *Paradise*
Nonfiction: "I was five years old the first time I ever set foot in prison." —Jimmy Santiago Baca, *A Place to Stand*

3. Philosophical

Fiction: "Happy families are all alike; every unhappy family is unhappy in its own way." —Leo Tolstoy, *Anna Karenina*
Nonfiction: "It's not about you." —Rick Warren, *the Purpose Driven Life*

4. Poetic

Fiction: "When I finally caught up with Abraham Trahearne, he was drinking beer with an alcoholic bulldog named Fireball Roberts in a ramshackle joint just outside of Sonoma, California, drinking the heart right out of a fine spring afternoon. —James Crumley, *The Last Good Kiss*

Nonfiction: "The village of Holcomb stands on the high wheat plains of western Kansas, a lonesome area that other Kansans call 'out there.'" —Truman Capote, *In Cold Blood*

Great opening lines from other classics may give you ideas for yours who said you can't copy one and modify.

Lesson 16: Your story should be
filled with conflict and tension

Your reader craves conflict; this applies to nonfiction readers as well.

In a novel, if everything is going well and everyone is agreeing, your reader will soon lose interest and find something else to do—like watch a Tv program rather than waste time reading your novel

Are two of your characters talking at a business meeting? Have one say something that makes the other storm out. Some deep-seeded rift in their relationship has surfaced. Is it just a misunderstanding that has snowballed into an injustice?

Thrust people into conflict with each other; just make your characters show some funny and mischievous moves. That'll keep your reader's attention.

Certain nonfiction genres won't lend themselves to that kind of conflict, of course, but you can still inject tension by setting up your reader for a payoff in later chapters by introducing new ideas and new ways of doing things. Check out some of the current bestselling nonfiction works to see how writers accomplish this. Somehow they keep you turning those pages and begging for more, even in a simple how-to title.

Tension is the secret sauce that will propel your reader through to the end, it what will keep them begging for more. And sometimes that's as simple as implying something to come. Not mastery the act of this could mean goodbye to your book and am sure you wouldn't want that.

Lesson 17: Don't worry your first draft can be a piece of crap

If you are a perfectionist like me you will find it hard to get a first draft written—fiction or nonfiction—without feeling compelled to make every sentence exactly the way you want it. That voice in your head that questions every word, every phrase, every sentence, and makes you worry you're being redundant or have allowed clichés to creep in—well, that's just your editor alter ego. He or she needs to be told to shut up that's just the solution, shut your editor self out if not you will never be satisfied with what you have written and it mean you aren't going anywhere.

You cannot be both creator and editor at the same time.
If you think otherwise, your first draft of even one brief chapter could take days to complete.
Our job when writing that first draft is to get down the story or the message or the teaching—depending on your genre.
A cliché, a redundancy, a hackneyed phrase comes tumbling out of my keyboard, and I start wondering whether I've forgotten to engage the reader's senses or aimed for

his emotions. That's when I have to chastise myself and say, "No! Don't worry about that now! First thing tomorrow you get to tear this thing up and put it back together again to your heart's content! I have edited my first draft over 20 times so why worry about getting a perfect job"

Imagine yourself wearing different hats for different tasks, if that helps— whatever works to keep you rolling on that rough draft. You don't need to show it to your worst enemy or even your dearest love. This chore is about creating. Don't let anything slow you down trying to become a perfectionist with your first draft is a dangerous one.
Some like to write their *entire* first draft before attacking the revision. As I say, whatever works for you is okay. Doing it that way would make me worry I've missed something major early that will cause a complete rewrite when I discover it months later.

I put my perfectionist hat on and grab my keyboard and trim that piece of work until I'm happy with every word.
Then I switch hats, tells Perfectionist Me to take the rest of the day off, and I start producing rough pages again. So, for me, when I've finished the entire first draft, it's actually a second draft because I have already revised and polished it in chunks every day. Then I go back through the entire manuscript one more time, scouring

it for anything I missed or omitted, being sure to engage the reader's senses and heart, and making sure the whole thing holds together.
I do not submit anything I'm not entirely thrilled with. I know there's still an editing process it will go through at the publisher, but my goal is to make my manuscript the absolute best I can before they see it.

Compartmentalize your writing vs. your revising and you'll find that frees you to create much more quickly.

Lesson 18: Stay put till you are done

Most people who fail at writing a book gave up somewhere along the way. That's a particularly rough stretch for novelists who have a great concept, a stunning opener, and they can't wait to get to the dramatic ending. But they bail when they realize they don't have enough cool stuff to fill the middle. They start padding, trying to add scenes just for the sake of bulk, but they're soon bored and know readers will be too.

This actually happens to nonfiction writers too. The solution there is in the outlining stage, being sure your middle points and chapters are every bit as valuable and magnetic as the first and last. If you strategize the progression of your points or steps in a process depending on nonfiction genre—you should be able to eliminate the strain in the middle chapters.

For novelists, know that every book becomes a challenge a few chapters in.

The shine wears off, keeping the pace and tension gets harder, and it's easy to run out of steam. But that's not the time to quit. Force yourself back to your structure, come up with a subplot if necessary, but do whatever you need to so your reader stays engaged.

Fiction writer or nonfiction author, at this point where you want to quit you must remember why you started this journey in the first place and how many times and people you told you were a writer. And it isn't just that you want to be an author. You have something to say. You want to reach the masses with your message.

Yes, it's hard. It still is for me every time. But don't panic or do anything rash, like surrendering. Embrace the challenge of the middle as part of the process. If it were easy, anyone could do it that's why everyone cannot.

❖ ❖ ❖

Lesson 19: Give a remarkable ending

Giving your book a remarkable ending is just as important for your nonfiction book as your novel. It may not be as dramatic or emotional, but it could be especially if you're writing a memoir.

But even a how-to or self-help book needs to close with a resounding thought, the way a Broadway theater curtain meets the floor.

How do you ensure your ending doesn't fizzle?

• Don't rush it. Give readers the payoff they've been promised.

They've invested in you and your book the whole way; take the time to make it satisfying I hate books that their ending fizzle, I sometime outline my ending even before starting the writing process although it does change.

• Never settle for close enough just because you're eager to be finished. Wait till you're thrilled with every word, and keep revising until you are complete empty.

• If it's unpredictable, it had better be fair and logical so your reader doesn't feel cheated. You want him to be delighted with the surprise, not tricked.

• If you have multiple ideas for how your book should end, go for the heart rather than the head, even in nonfiction. Readers most remember what moves them.

Lesson 20: Get a mentor

Get help from someone who's been where you want to be. That's the cheapest road to success Imagine engaging a mentor who can help you sidestep all the amateur pitfalls and shave years of painful trial-and-error off your learning curve. Just make sure it's someone who really knows the writing and publishing world.

Many people are parading the street as mentors and coaches but have never really succeeded themselves. Look for someone widely-published who knows how to work with agents, editors, and publishers.

There are many helpful mentors online that you can get for your book.

CHAPTER 3

Lesson 21: Your expectations

The writing business isn't a joke, now you have pass the hurdles involved in writing that your first book that almost took you up to three to four years or more to write, now that you are done and it is ready for publication, If I can peep into your heart I see that you have greats hopes and big expectations, well this little pages I call a book is set to reveal all you need to know about this part you have chosen, and am not here to be your friend, am here to tell you what I tag the real truth about publishing, the absolute truth.

Lower those expectations.

Now you are done with that book, the first truth to this is that you should lower your expectations. It is easy for people to say isn't it writing? I can write and anyone can write, that is true but I want to tell you this, Feel free to write the most beautiful, thought-provoking words using the language of your choice or in the basic language. The public will feel equally free to ignore them, it is a two way thing what you think and what the public think at the end it is what the public think that count.

Here's the sad truth: most people who write a book will never get it published, which is shocking write? But that is the hard truth, half the writers who are published won't see a second book in print talk more of a third book, and most books published are never reprinted. What's more, half the titles in any given bookshop won't sell a single copy there, and most published writers won't earn anything from their book apart from the advance.

So don't expect anything from your writing apart from the personal fulfillment of having learned your craft and created a work that didn't exist before, having the fulfillment of I started this book and completing it should be the only reward you got to expect after publishing your books if you don't want to be shocked and at the same time depressed, yours truly, failed expectations have a way of creating huge anxiety that later that can result depression. By all means hope to get published, and dream of having a bestseller or even a long string of them – people do, after all, and these people don't have two head they are like you and I, the only difference is that they polished their skills. But writing talent isn't nearly enough; you need more than just knowing how to pen down your ideas and imaginations, thousands of people have it, so there is nothing special about having the gift or talent of writing.

What do you do?

To succeed, you have to write the best story you possibly can, for the genre you're writing on, either fiction, non-fiction etc, and be professional in every other way. Many other industries work hard at their crafts but It is the writers who work hardest at every aspect of their craft because you are trying to bring the reader into your realm of imagination, so the writers and never give up, and it is the writer that doesn't give up that get there. And when you do, enjoy the adventure while it lasts, but don't expect it to last forever. It probably won't, am sure you have seen bunch of talented musicians in their prime, they were as if they could never be overtaken but as time goes on they had to give way to the newbie's who seems to understand what the audience need although not intentionally same applies to writers.

A rare few will ignore all this and succeed, but they're the lottery winners, most of you love to use the word lucky, sure they are the lucky winners and if you go with the mindset of being among the lucky winner I bet that you will be disappointed because most of the lottery winners never expected it. Everyone else has to work at it. Here me loud and clear, just don't expect too success or you're bound to be disappointed in this industry. Publishers are in business for the long term and they have to make a

profit. If you write books that sell, your publisher will love you. If you don't, its goodbye, no matter how much she or he likes your writing the winning game is sales and who wouldn't love such a writer that writes stories that sells?

Lesson 22: How to get your books published faster

It may surprise you to know that in this country, the big publishers each receive 4-5,000 unsolicited fiction manuscripts a year? That's around a hundred a week. Well you would have thought that the situation is different outside this country, but unfortunately the situation is much the same in the UK, Canada and the US – the only difference being that the bigger countries have more publishers which is a plus to writers.

Publishing is a competitive business, and no publisher can afford to pay people to read manuscripts. Some publishers no longer look at unsolicited manuscripts – they simply return them if postage is provided, that is if you were charged or shred them if it isn't. Where they do look at manuscripts, it will only be the professionally presented ones – perhaps half the total. Of that 2,500, say 90% will be rejected on the first page and 98% by the end of the first chapter. That leaves 30-50 manuscripts, and they're the only ones which will get any kind of serious consideration. In a good year, ten of those might be published, in a bad year, less than five.

Most published books come through agents these days, but no agent can afford to spend a lot of time reading manuscripts from unknown's authors. Most agents won't even look at an unsolicited manuscript and again, most manuscripts an agent does consider will be rejected on the first page and the reason for this you will find out in a little while.

Why does this agent reject manuscripts and those received rejected at most on the second page?

The lesson is obvious: your story has to start in the first paragraph, with an interesting character facing some kind of problem that captures the reader's interest or concern, and your very best writing has to be up front. Once you've done that, work on your contacts because agents get most of their manuscripts from referrals – it's the only practicable way to filter out the few good books from the vast morass of manuscripts that aren't publishable. Before you send your work off, make sure you present it in standard manuscript format which I have told you. If you don't, it's likely to be discarded without another glance.

How do you get your work on front of agents or editor?

- ❖ Writers' workshops and festivals.
- ❖ Other places where the industry gets together.
- ❖ Make contacts at book fairs.

Then use them

But how do you get your work in front of that agent or editor in the first place? Make contacts at book fairs, writers' workshops and festivals, and other places where the industry gets together, attending book fair is as important as writing your books. I mean what is the use of many written books without getting them to a publisher? After you have gathered enough contact then use them. Write to your contacts with your idea and perhaps a couple of sample pages (the first pages, obviously). If they like what they see, your manuscript is now a solicited one. It still won't be published if it's no good, but at least it's at the top of the queue to be read.

◆ ◆ ◆

WHAT IS MANUSCRIPT?

It refers to old documents actually written by hands.

It refers to a writer unpublished work whether it is typed or hand written.

It is your work of fiction or nonfiction you summit to a publisher or agent to be turned into a published book.

It is a book that is written for a submission to a publisher. Example of a manuscript is the author's copy of a book that the author has just turned in to the publisher to be published.

Standard format for manuscripts.

The standard format is the same format for essays and research paper works written in academic settings.

The Modern Language Association (MLA) specifies a standard format for essays and research papers written in academic setting as one-inch page margins. Double-space paragraphs.

A header with the author's last name.

Page number one-half inch from the top of each page.

Here are some of the standards.

- ❖ Use 12- point type.

- ❖ Use a serif font; I always recommend Times Roman.

- ❖ Double space your manuscripts.

- ❖ Avoid extra space between paragraphs.

- ❖ Give only once space between sentences.

- ❖ Indent each paragraph half an inch (setting a tab, not using several spaces)

- ❖ Make sure your text are flush left and ragged right, please not justified.

- ❖ Use black text on a white background only.

- ❖ One-inch margins (the default in Microsoft word)

- ❖ Create a header with the title followed by your last name and the page number. The header should appear on each page after the title page.

- ❖ Your agent and publishers want your name, email, address, and phone number even if they don't ask in the top right of your title page.

- ❖ *Your title should be about a third of your page.*

❖ *It should be the same size and font as the rest of the text; you shouldn't make it bold, italic or larger either. Point to note:*

❖ *Agent and publishers may sometimes have slightly different guidelines when it comes to how they want their manuscripts. Some will tell you a specific format they want e.g. The Chicago Manual of Style or the Associate Press.*

❖ *If they gave you the style they want give them.*

❖ *When they don't give you specification they want the standard manuscript but make sure you are consistent in your format.*

❖ *To make your work look professional follow certain general rules.*

Lesson 23: Your books are rejected?
This is what you need to do

Once you've done all that, and been rejected, send your work to another publisher right away. After all, it's just one editor's opinion and what one editor hates, another may love, this is a lifelong principle and it applies to writing and publishing too. If you've sent it to seven publishers and they've all rejected it, it's time to rewrite it. If you've sent it to fifteen, chuck it away and start again. If forty, assuming you can find that many publishers in your country write something else and change your name, writers are smart people you should learn how to be smart.

To experience the extraordinary diversity of opinions any work will get, check out the reader reviews, for any book you know well, on Amazon.com. Some will make you laugh and forget your sorrow, take a look at what sixty-odd readers say about my first book. One reader will attack the book, the author, editor, proof-reader, publisher and everyone else associated with it, as if mere publication of that book was a personal insult. The next reader will say it's the best book they've ever read.

Don't take rejection to heart. I once had my editor knock back a manuscript as 'un-publishable'. A fortnight later my agent sold it to another publisher for lots of money, they offered me a three-book contract into the bargain, and the book went on to get nice reviews in the UK and US who said you can't be the lucky one if you call that luck.

Lesson 24: Why your books might never get published

If you're continually being rejected after all your effort and all you have learnt here, I assume this was before this book was ever in your hand, it's time for ruthless self-analysis. These are the most common reasons that fiction manuscripts are rejected and I believe publishers might have different reasons:

❖   The writer simply can't write;

The writer has written a first draft and submitted it without bothering to edit it. No professional would submit a first draft; I know what it takes to edit a draft to a finite standard, in fact that is one part of this writing job that can frustrate you entirely and I don't usually blame editors for charging what they charge for editing.

Always do well to edit your draft or better still find an editor before sending it to a publisher.

❖   The storyline and characters are directly recycled from well known novels, TV shows, movies or computer games;
What most writers fail to understand is that if there is a movie for the book nobody bothers to read the book. So writing about a movie you watch or a TV series you so much enjoyed is way out of it if you ever wish to get published.
❖   It's not a story, just a series of unrelated events; or it's a polemic or rant, or a poorly disguised religious tract. No publisher will waste his or her time publishing a draft that the storylines are weird and out of this world.

❖   It's grossly violent, libelous, pornographic, depraved or offensive, or off-the-planet weird;

❖   It's not appropriate for the publisher you sent it to, or their publishing schedule is already full.

❖   The public simply aren't buying that kind of stuff at the moment.
This is a major factor why most books will not be published. Writing what isn't selling anymore or what readers aren't interested about will be a wasted effort and your publisher is too wise to make that mistake of publishing your book.

Even after you have written down what you consider your best though, make use of your friends, kids, family and listen to them. Listen to what people are telling you about your work. If you do have talent, take the advice of professionals and you'll immediately have an edge over most of your competitors, because few unpublished writers are really willing or able to act on criticism.

Lesson 25: You have been offered a contract, don't rush

As a novice writer, if a respectable publisher offers you a book contract, sign it. The chance may not come again. As a novice, you're not worth much to a publisher, so you have little power to negotiate your offer. If you demand a lot of changes to a contract, or cause interminable delays, the publisher may withdraw the offer and go to the next writer on their list. After all, a writer who causes trouble before the contract is signed is bound to be an even bigger pain afterwards and no publisher will see trouble ahead and gladly walk into one.

By all means ask your agent about the contract before you sign, and then take her advice. Be very wary about taking the contract to your solicitor, this is a mistake most novice publishers make. Few lawyers know anything about book contracts or the realities of publishing. If they get involved, they'll probably lose you the contract then bill you for most of the advance you didn't get and I bet that you don't want that.

If you haven't got an agent, get one now; it's easy once you have an offer from a publisher. Publishers have to be hard-headed businessmen, but they tend to think of authors as amateurs who should be grateful to be published at all. If you're equally hard-headed they may see you as aggressive and hard to deal with, which is counterproductive to a good working relationship. Let your agent do the hard-headed stuff while you be the nice, creative one who is after all, giving them the product they require to stay in business, and everyone will be happy.

Agents normally take 15% but she'll earn back her commission so she costs you nothing, and she may negotiate a few small extras. Once she's done a deal for you, she's entitled to her percentage of all income earned from that deal for as long as it lasts, even if you subsequently change agents. For foreign rights or special deals (e.g. movie rights – as if!), she'll work through other agents who also get a percentage.

Once you've got an agent, never talk directly to your publishers or editors about contractual matters, doing that is dangerous. You could disastrously undermine negotiations your agent is having with them, e.g. your agent is negotiating hard for a $20,000 advance and you've just told your editor you'd be happy with $10,000. Bad move!

Even your agent cannot go round that table with your publisher.

*Lesson 26: Why your book represent
a risk to your publisher*

Every new book represents a risk to the publisher, who is gambling tens of thousands of dollars that it will sell enough copies to earn a profit. Most books barely cover their costs or at best earn a small profit, and this is particularly the case with books by unknown authors it's just like a new business in town with the same product. Therefore, publishers have to keep costs down by offering small advances.

An advance is just that – an advance against future royalties – and the author doesn't get any money from book sales until the advance has been earned back by royalties from sales. The advance is seldom more than half to two-thirds of what the publisher expects the book to earn in royalties, insurance in case it does badly. As an example, say the book retails for $20 (plus tax), the author's royalty rate is 10% and the publisher expects to sell 5,000 copies. If it does, the book would earn the author $20 X 0.10 X 5,000, i.e. $10,000 in royalties. The publisher would normally offer an advance of between $5,000 and $7,000 and the balance would be paid in royalties at a later date. Despite that policy, a lot of books don't earn back their advances. A few years ago, two of the biggest international publishers had to write off tens of millions of dollars in unearned advances.

Most book advances in Australia, the UK and the US are less than $10,000. Surprisingly, most advances in the UK and US aren't a lot higher than here, despite the much bigger markets. Why not? There are a lot more titles published a lot more competition and, in the case of the US, much more fragmented markets.

If you're writing children's fiction, advances are typically lower than the figure I've quoted, despite the Harry Potter phenomenon. The reason – kid's books sell for a lower price. Partly offsetting that, the ones that do well can stay in print for a long time. For literary fiction, which may get the reviews and the awards but doesn't sell well, expect advances to be lower again: maybe only $1,000 – $3,000.

When you finally get the advance, don't spend it on something wasteful like food, clothing or rent. You're going to need every penny to promote your book; because the chances are that no one else will.

Lesson 27: what is good for you as an unknown author is a moderate advance

We all dream about the million dollar advance but, believe me you; if you're unknown you're better off with a moderate one. Huge advances create huge expectations and as an unknown author there's a good chance your sales won't meet expectations, in which case you're probably doomed, well the truth is until you actually published your book before you will really understand this point. Once booksellers get a whiff of declining sales, they'll start returning your books, and if they're not in the bookshops no one will be able to buy them. Then, because your first book flopped the bookshops won't order many of the second (if there is one), guaranteeing that it'll sell even less, the reason is simple no one will waste money into what or who is not bring more money, the law of asset and liability plays out here too .

Example. Suppose the publisher gives you a $50,000 advance for your first book, thus expecting it to sell at least, say, 40,000 copies. Unfortunately, despite lots of promotion, it only sells 10,000 copies. The publisher has done their dough and they and the booksellers will see you as a loser. You'll find it hard to sell a second book to that publisher. If another publisher does pick up your second book, you'll be lucky to get a $10,000 advance and orders will be much lower.

Instead, suppose the publisher advances you $10,000 for your first book 1/5 of the previous stated amount. If it sells 6,000 copies they're in the money. If it reprints a few times and sells 15,000 copies they'll love you and offer a much bigger advance for your second book. The bookshops will increase their orders and display your books prominently, and there'll be a small buzz about you in the industry. Do that two or three times and you're a rising star dancing in thousands or millions of dollars.

Lesson 28: Why you don't want
a tiny advance either

A tiny advance is a vote of no confidence in your work; and nobody wants that, it means the publisher isn't risking much on you, and therefore won't need to spend a lot of money on promotion, when this happened that might suggest you are already if not a failure going to fail. The promotional budget for your book is, generally, directly related to the size of the advance. So if you are offer a tiny advance common sense should suggest to you that your publisher is never going to get sweaty over your piece of literary work.

On the other hand, you have the opportunity, by your own clever promotional initiatives, to have a significant impact on sales. If the publisher is hoping to sell 4,000 copies and you can get that up to 6,000, they'll be very impressed. Publishers love authors who work hard to sell their books, and you'll get a better deal next time, and more promotion. And as an unknown author I don't see who will give you a huge advance so I advice you work hard to up your game by given all you have into promoting your books.

Lesson 29: The wise editor and the fool writer

Don't believe all that nonsense and crap you read about books not being edited any more. My editors put many weeks of work into each of my books, and always have. One of the best things about being published is having the opportunity to craft and polish your work with the aid of an experienced, sensitive professional. I know you might say I don't know where to get an editor? Thank God for the internet again, you can get an editor within seconds of typing the word editor on Google but fiverr freelancing platform accessible by fiverr.com is a perfect place to start from, you can get an editor on fiverr for as low as $5.

Editors are overworked and underpaid, but they know a lot more about writing and the marketplace than you do remember a lot of people just start writing with the believe that they are talented enough but nobody is an editor by talent, if you are one then you are the first I'm seeing editor spent hours and time in their lives trying to study and get knowledge about their craft except for those pirated guys out there just hustling, and they're usually right. Consider carefully every point your editor makes it might save you thousands of dollars you would have lost to low sales. Where you reject an editorial suggestion, make sure there's a good reason for it. I would agree with 9 out of 10 suggestions my editor makes. If you're rejecting most of them, you've got a problem. In rare cases an editor may be wrong for your book, but more likely the problem is that you can't accept criticism. In that case, kiss your writing career goodbye no offence I said I was going to tell you the truth.

Beginning writers have less leeway than established ones. An established writer can ignore most of her editor's suggestions and still be published (though few would be so unprofessional). A novice who does so may never be published is as simple as that. If your editor tells you to cut your 1000 page manuscript to 500 pages, do it. Cutting a long book almost invariably makes it better. Big books cost a lot more to edit, print and distribute, but a publisher can't charge much more for them. That's OK if they're by a bestselling author, but it's a recipe for losing money if they're the work of a novice.

Once you've had a few books published, your editor's comments will fall into a familiar pattern – an introductory paragraph of effusive praise followed by many pages of detailed comments and suggestions. Don't let the praise go to your head – she's not going to rubbish a book the publisher has already paid good money for. Neither get too downcast about the cumulative effect of all those critical comments. They're intended to make the book better and, after all, the publisher has paid good money for it, and must think it's a goal.

Your manuscript will generally go through two stages of editing. The structural edit largely looks at the big picture, the central idea of your writing after which you do your major revisions, then there's the copy edit (or line edit), which attends to the line by line details. Some publishers frown on the author making significant changes at the line edit stage. Get the book right during editing, because major changes at the proof stage (i.e. after it's been typeset) are very expensive. If you insist on rewriting your proofs, you may have to pay for the changes and they won't be cheap.

If you're published in more than one country, you may have to deal with a number of editors. British publishers are often happy with Australian editing; American publishers will want to change the spelling, at least, but may also re-edit the story to suit the sensitivities of the US market, or their own editorial concerns. This can cause problems if they're undoing changes you've made to suit

your original editor. On the other hand, it's better than not being published there at all.

Lesson 30: Printing your books

There's a lot that goes on behind the scenes that you don't know about and publishers like to have the manuscript ready for editing 9-12 months before the publication date. Your publisher won't schedule the publication date until she has the manuscript in hand, because late changes to the schedule are inconvenient, embarrassing and expensive. If your book is scheduled for October, say, to take advantage of the pre-Christmas sales period, and you deliver a month too late, publication is likely to be delayed for months because you aren't the only one on their schedules. The publisher's schedule is set at least six months in advance and there may not be an available slot for you to be published in November. Few books are published in December or January, and Febrary is the slowest sales month of the year. Furthermore, promotional opportunities such as space in booksellers' catalogues may already be booked up, so if you miss your chance you may not get another.

About 20 milestones have to be met in the production of your book, including:

Book design (including cover design, layout and typography)

Editing (several stages)

Typesetting and proofreading (3 stages)

Cover brief and preparation of cover art (3 or more stages)(sometimes a number of cover roughs will be produced. It's not uncommon for a cover to be rejected during this process and a new cover concept formulated or even for a new artist to be commissioned) several program meetings to keep key people up to date

Cover copy

Marketing

Sales brief

Cover proof and printing

Text printing and binding

Delivery to warehouse (usually a month before publication date)

Delivery of initial orders to the bookshops in time for publication date

In an emergency, e.g. for a really topical book or a blockbuster author who delivers late, all this can be done in two months. For everyone else, where a book is to be published in, say, October, this process would begin in January or February, after the manuscript has been accepted and editing is underway, and be completed in late August when finished books are delivered to the

warehouse. In a publishing house, decisions to approve these milestones are normally made in meetings, not by individuals.

Australian and British publishers will generally consult you about the covers, though they won't necessarily adopt your suggestions, which is fine. They ought to know what constitutes a good cover in their marketplace. American publishers may not consult you at all, which isn't as bad as it sounds. American covers are so different to Australian and British ones that you may not have anything useful to contribute. e.g., American fantasy covers without people on them rarely succeed, whereas to the Australian and British eye such covers often look cute or twee. Australian or British publishers may ask you to provide copy for the blurb. American publishers will probably write their own and may change the title to suit their own sensibilities or markets.

CHAPTER 4

Lesson 31: You're not published
until it is over

Deals fall over for all sorts of reasons, so don't count your chickens until they're roosting in a thousand bookshops. Here are some of the most common problems.

There was a 'misunderstanding' when the publisher made your agent an offer for your book. You don't get a publishing contract after all, or you get a contract but a worse deal than originally offered.

The publisher goes bankrupt before your book is published. If they've paid the advance, you keep it. If they haven't, you're back in the queue.

Your editor leaves or is fired and her replacement hates your book and decides not to publish it. You keep the advance though.

The publisher is having a tough time and decides that they would lose money publishing your book. You keep

the advance and, if you're lucky, they might pay you a small sum in lieu.

The editor loves your book and offers a terrific hardcover deal and great promotion, but the sales department or the major book buyers don't agree that it has big sales potential. You get down-graded to paperback, with little or no promotion, and your potential income and sales are massively reduced.

Your book is found to be libelous and the publisher doesn't want to get sued, so they cancel publication, or if it's been printed, withdraw the book and pulp it. You've violated your contract and have to pay back the advance, and they could even sue you for their losses.

Your non-fiction book is proven to be fraudulent, ditto.

❖ ❖ ❖

Lesson 32: Put your money where your manuscript is

If all else fails and you're really sure that you've written a good book, there's one resort left – publishing it yourself. This isn't easy, and it definitely isn't cheap, but if you've got months to spare and at least $10,000 lying around with nothing to spend it on, you could consider self-publishing, I self published my first book. Two of Australia's best selling writers began that way, and many other writers have in other countries.

But the vast majority of self-publishers do their dough, so if you are going to do it, do it right, and get the right advice, otherwise you might as well tear your money up and flush it down the toilet. You must employ a professional editor, a professional cover designer and have the book typeset. This will cost you $5,000 – $6,000, or more if your book is long and requires a lot of editing. Printing will cost you another $4,000 – $6,000, or more if it's long or you have a lot of copies printed.

Don't print more than 500. The biggest problem of all is distribution, which is why publishers have invested millions in it. It takes the most monumental effort for an individual to sell more than 300 – 400 copies, even if you get some good publicity and a few bookshops stock your books. Print too many and they'll still be rotting in your garage in a decade always start small and then grow.

Lesson 33: Is that all you're printing?

Your favorite author gets a 200,000 copy print run, but don't even dream about doing the same, I don't need to remind you that you are a novice to everyone. He's spent 20 years building his name and sales. And besides, he got in first, and lots of other authors in your chosen genre have prospered since, so there's not much room in the market for newcomers these days.

Print runs are surprisingly low in Australia and other English speaking countries – in fact everywhere. The initial paperback print run for a popular fiction title by a new author in Australia would typically be 3,000 – 8,000 copies. For literary fiction, it might only be 1,000 – 2,000 copies. In the UK, initial paperback print runs for popular fiction by new authors are typically 10,000 or less, and in the US, 25,000 or less. Again, for literary novels, print runs can be considerably lower. If you sell translations, print runs for European countries, except the largest, are likely to be in the range 1-4,000 copies.

In Australia, only major best sellers are published in hardcover because consumers are reluctant to pay for them. It's much the same in the UK. A lot of authors are published in hardcover in the US, where it's a sign that your publisher is enthusiastic about your book. Even there, typical hardcover print runs are 10,000 or less.

Lesson 34: you are disappointed
after it was printed

Rare authors fall in love with their book once it's published, but more common are feelings of self-consciousness, embarrassment or even mortification. The tiniest flaws now appear gigantic, while the typos, errors and inconsistencies that no one noticed during editing and proofreading are numerous and glaringly obvious it happens to almost everybody.

Don't expect adulation. The public has a curious attitude to authors – those who know how small most book sales are will display a pitying admiration for you, because you're doing what you love even though you can't make any money at it. Others confuse 'published author' with 'famous author' and assume you're stinking rich. Either way, take what pleasure you can – after all, you are doing what you love and thousands of people are just aching to get there themselves.

Don't expect your brand new book to be stocked by every bookshop (chapter 1 lesson 1) much less displayed promineintly. If it's in the shop at all, there's a good chance it'll be shelved spine-out and practically invisible. Neither expects bookshop staff to recognize your name when you drop in to say hi. Hundreds of books will have come in that month and they probably won't recognize yours, or know what to say to you. It'll be different once you've got a few books out and your name is familiar; they'll be glad to see you then because few writers drop into bookshops to say hello. But take some leaflets showing your book cover anyway, as a reminder.

And if you have a book launch or a signing, don't expect a lot of people to come unless you round up all your friends and relatives.

The average number of people at a book signing in the US is four, and it's much the same here (though you'll generally do a lot better in towns than in the capital cities). That doesn't mean book signings aren't worthwhile; your books get good display space and promotion, and the shop will sell quite a few of them over the next few weeks (especially if you sign them.

Lesson 35: Promoting your book.

Facts you should know about sales and promotion:

❖ Sales and marketing are both very expensive, and most books aren't going to sell enough copies to justify muchmore than the minimum expenditure (i.e. an entry in the monthly sales catalogue).

❖ Promotion doesn't increase the size of the market – all it can do is influence people to spend their money on your book rather than someone else's book.

❖ The most effective form of promotion is in-bookshop, so the first aim is to get as many of your books as possible into the shops, prominently and enticingly displayed. If your publisher can't get the bookshops to stock them, the chances of the public buying many are low.

❖ It takes a lot of work (and money) behind the scenes to get bookshops to stock a new author's book in quantities – this includes good book design, an attention-grabbing cover and blurb, quotes ('puff pieces') from relevant authors, reviewers or celebrities and, if you're lucky, a well-thought-out marketing and promotional campaign to draw the public's attention to the book.

If you're really lucky, the publisher might do a limited run of proof copies in the hope that key book buyers will make big orders and influential reviewers provide flattering quotes before publication.

Fiction is much harder to promote than non-fiction, and for every author whose name has been successfully promoted, there are several for whom promotion (some

times heaps of it) has simply failed to capture the public's attention.

Advertising will help if it's properly targeted, but it's very expensive and needs to be repeated a lot to make much difference I have spent over $20 without making a single sales that's how crazy it can be sometimes (the Rule of Seven applies, i.e. people need to be reminded about seven times before it sinks in). Word of mouth is king. That's why, when a new movie comes out, by Saturday night everyone in the country knows whether it's hit or a dog. It's the same with your book, though it normally takes months to get word of mouth going. More often it's years and a number of books.

It's really difficult to promote an author that no one has ever heard of and if you do get some free publicity, it won't sell many books. For a new author, even a feature article in a capital city newspaper would be lucky to sell a hundred books. (The same-sized article about a big name author might sell a thousand copies plus swag of backlist.) Ditto with radio interviews – it's important to do

them, but even if you do twenty or thirty it may only sell a few hundred books. Do them anyway – those sales could be the difference between success and failure, and it all helps in the essential task of building awareness about you – the vital recognition factor, when you are getting familiar you are moving up the scale at least you are no longer that author you were yesterday some few people are getting to know you.

To become a successful author, you have to establish your name as a brand that the reading public can trust. If they spend twenty bucks on your book, they expect to get their money's worth of entertainment. If they don't, your readers will feel ripped off and tell their friends what a rotten book it was and that means bad business for you.

❖ ❖ ❖

Lesson 36: Do it yourself promotion

The publisher will generally produce some kind of a sales and marketing plan (which may include a promotional itinerary) for your book, but probably won't tell you about it unless you ask. Ask nicely but don't have a fit if they're not doing much. If the market for your book is small, there's no point in the publisher spending a lot on promotion. And ask to see their media release as well. You can usually improve it a lot, but remember that people in the media get dozens of press releases a day, so you've got about 20 seconds to attract their attention.

It's hard to know what's going to work and what isn't, and the secret of successful promotion is to do a lot of different things in the hope that some of them will be effective. A sales and marketing plan could include a number of the following, if you're lucky, though remember that they all cost money and often serious amounts of it:

Sales (by publisher's sales team)

a featured book in your publishers' sales catalogue and website, or even a special website for the author, book or series; sales pitches to: the trade (i.e. book chains) as well as mass market (discount stores, supermarkets, news agencies and airports), tele-sales, backlist sales to existing customers as well as book clubs and party-plan customers (i.e. home selling), export sales etc;

Educational sales and marketing;

Advertising (publisher's marketing group)

book chain advertising, e.g. as featured book in book chains' monthly catalogues or special or Christmas catalogues, or even as Book of the Month or Author of the Month (all these on publisher-pays basis); consumer advertising (print media, rail posters, com-petitions etc);

Promotion (publisher and yourself)

Retail promotion (introductory offer price, '3 for 2' or '2 for $30', and other price promotions; book chains' genre promotions);

Point of sale material (posters, dump bins, etc, though it can be hard to get bookshops to take these);

Publicity (typically radio and press interviews, book signings, launches, literary lunches, conference and literary festival ap-pearances school visits etc. Rarely TV appearances. although only if you're gorgeous or famous); giveaways for radio and print media competitions; and/or mail out of review copies to list of reviewers (can be 50 or more of these).

If the publisher can't afford to promote your book, get stuck into it yourself. You can't sell to bookshops and you can't afford advertising, but you can promote very effectively. After all, no one knows more about your work than you do, and all you have to do is talk enthusiastically about it to people who love books.

Since you weren't expecting publication, the advance should be treated as a windfall and spent promoting your book. Spend it wisely, but quickly. To have a chance of succeeding, your book has to sell a critical mass of copies in the first two months, to ensure that bookshops will be re-ordering and there'll be a positive buzz in the industry, rather than returning with it negative feelings; and hopefully, word of mouth from satisfied readers will keep your sales going long after the initial sales period.

Don't leave it too late. You've got to start at least a month before the books come out and be ready for your biggest push as soon as they're in the bookshops.

And whatever you're planning to do, make sure to keep you editor/publisher/agent/publicist informed. They need to know. It's also an important part of promoting yourself to them as an energetic author who really wants to push the books they've invested so much in.

Lesson 37: What happened to books that don't get reviewed?

If you expect your shiny new book to be reviewed in a major newspaper the week it comes out, or even in the six months after that, you're going to be cruelly disappointed. Most books never get reviewed and don't expect yours so soon, and it's easy to see why. Australia has more than 20,000 books published a year (10,000 being local titles), the UK around 120,000 (more than doubling in the past 25 years), and the US around 175,000 a year (though 150,000-odd also went out of print, thankfully). The major newspapers and periodicals have space to review only a tiny fraction of those books. Take out the duplication and only a few thousand books would get mainstream media coverage a year, of which most would be non-fiction, or by well-known novelists, or worse, celebrities.

That leaves hardly any space for novels by beginning writers and it's not going to change. Newspapers are written for a particular audience but a novice writer doesn't have one. The same goes for feature articles

and TV appearances, only more so. If you're young, female and beautiful, you've got a chance. Writers in other categories only get that kind of coverage once they're successful (for TV, really successful and articulate). The downside of being YF&B is that you tend to get dismissive, condescending publicity, often suggesting that you only got published because of your looks, this is reality am telling you.

The good news is that one review, even a big, glowing one, won't make a big difference to your book sales (and neither will a really bad one). To significantly bump sales up, you need reviews and articles in a good cross-section of the media, and that's unlikely before you've sold a truckload of books. One average-sized review in a big city paper might sell twenty or thirty books – a hundred if you're lucky. Besides, most people who read popular fiction don't read reviews. And don't expect to get glowing reviews – they're very rare. Don't get too upset about the stinkers, either. Ignore them and use the good ones – quotes on book covers do make a difference.

Lesson 37: What's a good sale?

Books are generally sold to bookshops on a 'sale or return' basis, meaning that any books they haven't sold after a specified period (typically three months or more) can be sent back for a credit. Unsold books aren't necessarily returned. Since this costs time, labour, freight etc, sometimes the bookshop may prefer to discount if they think the books are going to sell in a reasonable time. If not, back they go, Returns start coming in around the beginning of the fourth month (earlier in some cases) and most will have come back by 6-8 months, though some returns can still come in over a year later.

Returns in Australia average around 35% of initial orders, so if your returns are much lower than this you're doing well. If significantly above this figure your publisher will be worried. Returns in the UK and US are similar or higher (though the shelf life is likely to be shorter and, in the US, mass market paperbacks are such cheap editions that unsold copies are not worth returning).

Sometimes your publisher will do a deal to sell a new title to a book chain on a non-return basis, in exchange for a higher discount. These are guaranteed sales and therefore the bookshop will make extra efforts to shift them. They're easy to pick – the ones that have been marked down several times.

With trilogies and longer series, which are the rule in fantasy and some SF, the subsequent books will always sell less than the first. Readers who don't like the first book won't buy any more, while those who buy the second book will probably purchase the whole series. In a successful series, sales of the second book will typically be around 70% of the first. If the second book sells only half as many as the first, the series is in trouble. Somewhat lower percentages prevail in the UK and US, where there are a lot more titles available and hence more competition.

In Australia, sales of roughly 2,500+ in trade paperback are respectable and 5,000+ are good. In A-format (i.e. mass market paperback) the approximate figures are 4,000+ and 10,000+. Less than 200 books (in all formats, non-fiction as well as fiction) would sell more than 20,000 copies in a year.

In the UK, sales of 5,000+ in trade paperback are respectable and 10,000+ are good. In A-format the approximate figures are 8,000+ and 15,000+. Not very high, are they?

In the US, sales of 5,000+ in hardcover are respectable and 10,000+ are good. For mass market paperback, the approximate figures would be 15,000+ and 40,000+.

◆ ◆ ◆

Lesson 38: how long do you wait to get pay?

One of the bitter lessons of publication is how long you have to wait for the money, starting with the advance. Publishing is organized so that money advanced to the author is recovered as quickly as possible, while money owed to the author is retained as long as possible. The advance is normally paid in two or three stages:

❖   One-third 'on signing' (can be a couple of months after)
❖   One-third on 'delivery' of the completed manuscript (which actually means when your editor accepts it – this can be months of revisions later)
❖   One-third on publication

If you do a multi-book deal, the publisher may front-load the advance onto the first book's sales rather than spreading it across all three. Your agent should resist such contracts.

Should your books earn royalties or money from sales of various rights, you'll be paid these twice a year, three months after the end of the royalty period (i.e. for January to June sales you'll be paid at the beginning of October, and for July-December sales, at the beginning of April. Normally 20% of your royalties will be retained by the publisher in a 'reserve against returns', in case a lot of your books are returned by bookshops. Even if the initial print run has sold out and your book keeps selling, the publisher will retain this money for three royalty periods (18 months) because that's how the contract is written.

However you may be able to negotiate a top-up advance, to be paid in the event your sales earn back the advance within a short period.

Where income is earned from sales of other rights, foreign royalties etc, and the publisher will normally retain your share until the next royalty period, though you can request that they pay it earlier.

◆ ◆ ◆

Lesson 39: What happened to sales you don't get much for?

High discount sales done for promotional purposes

one of the reason you don't get much return, even on Amazon kindle authors are usually advice to give out a volume of their books for free in other to drag more traffic and make their books more visible to more readers.

To introduce you as a new author, e.g. if you get picked up by a major book chain as Author of the Month, the publisher may sell your books to that chain at a high discount in return for a large order, and guaranteed publicity and shelf space. In this case you may only get 80% or even 60% of the normal retail royalties, but it'll be worth it because it can double your initial sales and get your name exposed to the public quickly.

Export sales

Export sales are worth lot less than local sales, so always try to sell your book to a publisher in your own country first. If you sell your book to an US or UK publisher and they export them to Australia, you'll get, per book, about a third to a half of what you'd get from a book published in Australia and sold here (and a local publisher would

sell a lot more copies). But if you can't sell your book to a local publisher, the export sales are better than nothing.

Book clubs

Sales to book clubs are made at a very high discount, 75-80% of the normal retail price, and you'll receive

a correspondingly reduced royalty, typically about 45 cents for a trade paperback and 30 cents for a paperback. Such deals are worth it because they're sales you wouldn't otherwise get, and book clubs produce massive quantities of promotional leaflets which will help to gain you regular bookshop sales.

Readers Digest

A sale to Reader's Digest for their condensed books could be worth it because of the kudos and exposure for your name, and the sales you wouldn't otherwise get. They'll print 100,000 copies of your book in this country, maybe more. The royalty rate is very low, however, around 5 cents per book.

Special editions/omnibus editions etcOccasionally your publisher may make a deal with a particular book chain to do a special printing of one or more

of your books as an 'introductory offer', or other specially priced deal to increase your sales. You might only get 50-80 cents per book but you'll get good front-of-

the-shop exposure, extra sales and hopefully it'll also increase the sales of all your non-discounted books.

The same applies with omnibus editions of your books. You may only get 50 cents per book but you'll get thousands of extra sales. These promotional editions may increase your overall sales, or may come at the expense of your full-priced books. You won't know for at least a year.

Remainders

If your book is remaindered, you'll typically get 10% of the publisher's receipts, which will be around 30 cents per book (a bit more for hard covers or trade paperbacks). However, if remainders are sold at less than the cost of production (about two dollars a book) you won't get anything. Your publisher should offer remainders to you at the remainder price first, so buy as many as you can afford. They make great give-away.

Reprinted to be remainderedIf your print book has an enticing cover, it could be picked up by a book repackage person and reprinted for the '3 for $10' bins at the front of the bookshop. They'll do a big reprint (25,000 copies or more) a swag of which could be shipped overseas. The royalty rate will be about 5 cents per copy, but it may be worth it for the exposure of your name.

◆ ◆ ◆

*Lesson 40: Check your royalty
statements against your contract*

Every publisher's royalty statements are different and some aren't very informative. Some are almost incomprehensible, and rarely will any publisher's statement give you all the information you need, even though they have it at their fingertips. This is what your royalty statement should tell you, so you can be fully informed and manage your writing business properly:

Actual number of books received from the printer (usually a few percent higher than the nominal print run);

Stock at the beginning and end of the royalty period;

Sales in various categories, price received and royalty rate applied (e.g. for retail, discount, book club and other special sales, export sales);

Returns, promotional copies and other giveaways, faulty or damaged stock destroyed;

Income from foreign rights and royalties, and other rights sold (with exchange rates applying on the day of conversion);

Balance of your royalty account for each title (i.e. advances debited from it, and income from foreign rights, royalties or other rights' sales credited);

Amount of reserve-against-returns deducted and when it's to be repaid.

Check your royalty statements carefully. Mistakes are not uncommon and they'll rarely be in your favour. Some typical ones I've heard about:

The wrong royalty rate used (invariably lower than the applicable rate)

Advance or other contracted payments not made when due.

Royalties not paid even though advance has been earned back

Advance for a new book or multi-book contract applied to your royalty account for an existing book or multi-book contract, thus ensuring that you're not paid royalties owed.

Reserve against returns incorrectly subtracted from foreign rights income or from more than one edition of a particular book (unless contract allows the latter).

But don't you make mistakes either, e.g., don't complain that you've sold, say, 22,000 copies and you're not getting the higher royalty on sales over 20,000 K, without checking. The contract first, It will almost certainly say that the higher royalty rate applies on full-priced sales. Books sold at a high discount, i.e. where you get a reduced royalty rate, don't count towards the total.

CHAPTER 5

*Lesson 41: Other source of income
from your books*

In Australia, as in many other countries, you can be paid a small sum per book for copies of your books held in public libraries (PLR) and educational libraries (ELR). You have to register for both by filling in the form that your publisher will send you when your book is published. Payment is at a fixed rate for PLR (currently $1.37 per book held) and a reducing scale for ELR (average about $0.50 per book), based on a census of books in these libraries. Payment is deposited to your bank account in May and June respectively. Most writers would get from a few hundred to a few thousand dollars a year, but a rare few will get tens of thousands of dollars. Quite a few children's authors, however, who have written a large number of small books, will earn five figures from these rights.

By all means register with the Copyright Agency (CAL), which distributes payments for photocopying in institutions, though if you're writing popular fiction you probably won't earn anything from it.

❖   Cultural Gifts Program Australia, also in line with a number of other countries, has a Cultural Gifts Scheme to encourage creative artists in all fields to donate their works to Australian institutions rather than selling them on the world market. The scheme is administered by the Commonwealth Department of Communications, Information Technology and the Arts. First you need to find an institution that's willing to accept your works, which shouldn't be too hard if you're an established writer. A writer's works could include the various draft manuscripts of a work, plans, outlines and synopses, correspondence related to the work, emails, promotional material, copies of overseas editions etc.

The library will collect the works and have them valued at what they'd fetch on the world market (by two independent valuers). You'll subsequently get a tax deduction based on the average of the two values. The value of the material would typically be in the range $1,000 to $10,000 per book for established mid-range authors, though this would depend on whether they've had international success and whether the international marketplace would be interested in the genre. For example, science fiction and fantasy, being world literatures, are

probably worth more than books that are of only local interest.

For beginning writers, the program is worth little if anything. If you believe you're going to become a megastar, hang onto your material until you reach the peak of your career, when it may be worth a fortune.

❖   Arts Council And Other Literary Grants

If you're a novice writing popular fiction, don't waste your time applying for a grant. Grants go overwhelmingly to literary fiction writers. The only exception is for children's fiction.

If you've a number of books published, won an award or two and have had good reviews by important reviewers, you have a slim chance of getting a grant if you're writing popular fiction. Grants are hard to get and even literary writers have less than a 20% chance per application.

*Lesson 42: You won an award and
now you're being remaindered*

Your book had great reviews and won an award, but it only sold 1,200 copies and just two years after publication it's out of print. What's gone wrong?

There are two main kinds of awards – voted awards and judged awards. The former are voted on by the members of an organization (or at least by the 10-20% of members who actually vote). A number of SF awards are voted awards, e.g. the Hugo and Nebula Awards and, in Australia, the Ditmars. Such awards, like the Oscars, are given partly for quality and partly for popularity, so it helps to be well known and likeable (and to round up all your friends to vote so that you get on the shortlist. It can take surprisingly few votes to do this).

Judged awards are generally assessed by a panel of judges, usually from academia or literary figures. They tend to be looking for literary qualities, originality and themes that are of concern to them. These are often not the qualities that would appeal to the reading public.

The really big awards, such as the Children's' Book Council Book of the Year, the Miles Franklin, Carnegie Medal, Booker Prize, Hugo and Nebula Awards etc will make a big difference to your sales, and publishers will usually put out a new edition to capitalize on the win. Lesser awards, such as State literary awards, or genre awards like the Aurealis, won't have a significant impact on sales (and winning them may indicate that your writing is at the literary rather than the popular end of the spectrum). By the time your book is announced as the winner, there probably won't be a lot of copies left in the bookshops. If it is still available, stickers on the cover could sell a few hundred extra copies but you're unlikely to get a reprint out of it. You'll just have to be content with the warm glow of approbation from your peers.

Lesson 43: It takes years to become an overnight success

Success as a novelist requires you to establish your name, just like any other brand. That's going to take years of building sales by word of mouth from satisfied readers, so don't have unrealistic expectations about becoming a brilliant success overnight, if you have forgotten refer back to (Chapter 1 lesson 1). Building a successful writing career requires you to keep selling your backlist and, for most writers of popular fiction, that means writing some form of series that your readers can identify with and keep following over the years and it not always a piece of cake. Series can have a variety of forms, such as:

❖ Independent or loosely linked novels featuring the same character or characters (common in crime fiction, action/adventure, thrillers, military, children's fiction, some SF);
❖ Novels with the same general kind of story and setting, but with different characters (e.g. much romance writing; courtroom dramas);

❖ Multi-volume novels (trilogies, quartets and longer series) featuring a core of common characters engaged in a long project or quest (e.g. much if not most fantasy and some SF).

If you can write a compelling series with engaging, developing characters, each new book should build sales of your backlist. The big problem comes when you want to write something different as, sooner or later, you almost certainly will.

Lesson 44: The perils of success 1

No matter how successful you are in one genre, don't think you'll be able to transfer it to another. Few writers can. Your loyal readers want more of the same and they'll be unhappy if they don't get it. Switch genres and you can expect to lose 90% of your readers, no matter how good you are in the new genre. Why? The bookshops will be reluctant to order your new gritty thrillers if they know you as a writer of historical romances, your present readers won't buy them because that's not the kind of stuff they like to read, and new readers either haven't heard of you or know you as a romance writer, and they hate romance.

In any case, your present publisher is most unlikely to buy your new book, because she knows how difficult it will be to sell. Another publisher might – even 10% of your existing sales may be worth having if you're big enough – but won't pay much. If you really want to write

in a new genre you may be better off changing your name to avoid confusing everyone.

Even writing a new series within the same genre can lose you sales, if the style or characters are very different from the old series. But hey, you're not in it for the money but passion.

Alternatives:

You can slowly evolve your writing and hope to take existing readers with you. Some writers succeed, many do not.

Or write in other styles or genres early in your career, before you're typecast (if you can get them published).

Start a new series before you've finished the old one, to ease the transition.

Lesson 45: The perils of success 2

Many writers have only one or two books in them and, while a few writers have been successful writing the same book over and again, most fade away once they've nothing left to say.

Tastes change and styles date. What's quaint and quirky, or dazzlingly original, one year will be pass the next. Even genres boom and bust: westerns have practically disappeared, horror goes up and down like a roller coaster from decade to decade and SF seems to be in long term decline. And it's remarkable how few of the really big names of 20 years ago are still big today.

Luckily, one kind of writing never goes out of fashion – a good story well told, with well-drawn characters that the reader can identify with (if not necessarily like). But always remember that you're competing with all the other writers in your genre, in the world, and you're only as good as your last book.

The other thing you have to do is be productive. Most successful popular writers produce a book a year, if not more. One of the most successful of all, Nora Roberts, writes eight books a year but she is, of course, a phenomenon. New titles are the fuel that keeps your backlist sales going and, once you stop writing, even if you're a bestselling author now, your books will soon go out of print.

◆ ◆ ◆

Lesson 46: What's a bestseller?

U ntil recently, if a book made a bestseller list anywhere, anytime, the publisher would plaster 'Bestseller' across the front, but overuse has devalued the currency to meaninglessness. Furthermore, many bestseller lists excluded popular fiction in favour of literary works, and were widely manipulated.

Recently, with the advent of Book Scan which gathers point-of-sale data from 1000 retail outlets nationwide, the weekly bestseller lists have become a more reliable guide to what's actually selling. (The same company produces bestseller lists in the UK and US.) Strictly speaking, however, these aren't bestseller lists so much as 'fast seller' lists – books which sell a lot of copies in a short time. Some may go on to become genuine bestsellers, though many will have disappeared within a year or two. In most weeks of the year, you can get to No. 1 in Australia with sales of 3,500 copies, though the biggest title

just before Christmas might sell 40,000 copies in that week. the annual lists are a better guide to the true bestseller. In Australia, for adult hardcover, full priced sales of 7,500 copies in a year are required to make the annual APA bestseller list. For adult trade paperbacks, its 10,000 copies and for mass market adult paperbacks, 15,000 copies. Roughly 100 titles make each annual list. The biggest selling title in each of these categories would sell around a quarter of a million copies in the year (lifetime sales would be rather higher). The Harry Potter books sell around 800, 000 copies+ in a year.

In the UK, a new paperback can make the annual Guardian Fast seller Top 100 list with 175,000 copies (this generally includes substantial export copies) and the top seller will sell around a million copies in the year. The writers on this list are almost all British, Irish or American. While Australian writers do make the list from time to time, none has ever made the annual Top 100 consistently. The only other writer who does is Wilbur Smith (South Africa).

In the US, the number one adult fiction book of the year (on the Publisher's Weekly list) can sell as much as 5-6 million copies in hardcover. Thirty years ago the top figure was 300,000 copies; now more than fifty titles have hardcover sales over that figure. The top seller in trade paperback and mass market paperback is generally over two million each. Mass market paperback sales have declined significantly over the years, with loss of non-book-shop sales outlets, but hardcover sales have risen

dramatically as the price differential has fallen. Children's' hard-cover and paperback front list and backlist top sellers tend to be around a million copies each per year, except for the latest Harry Potter whose sales will be around 12 million. In each category, the top 100-150 children's titles will sell over 100,000 copies.

Many books that sell steadily for years may never make the best-seller lists, though they can end up selling a lot more copies than bestsellers that shone briefly only to be out of print a year or two later. In the US, 18 hardcover novels sold over 100,000 copies in 2003 without once making the weekly bestseller lists.

Lesson 47: Selling Foreign Rights.

If your books are big sellers in your own country, there's a good chance that you'll be able to sell foreign rights, though this depends on genre. Science fiction and fantasy are easily sold internationally. Romance and thrillers are harder to sell: less so if they're set in Europe or America, or in historical times; much more difficult if they're set in Australia. Crime set in Australia has a limited international market, as do most other forms of Australian literature.

Foreign rights deals can either be done by your publisher (typically for 20%) or by a foreign agent (10%) working with your local agent (15%). If your name isn't well known and your publisher is energetic, you might be better off with the publisher marketing your foreign rights. Your publisher has the resources to hawk your books at Frankfurt and the other big book fairs, and will already

have relationships with agents in many countries. This can also avoid foreign tax issues and payment problems (i.e. getting the money out of your foreign publisher). Some Australian publishers are extremely good at selling foreign rights, while others have little experience. Find out before signing a contract that allows your publisher to do these deals.

There are about 198 countries in the world, and thousands of languages, though only the literary superstars would be published in more than 20 countries. In general, foreign publishing rights aren't worth a great deal of money to the developing or mid-range novelist, although if you sell enough of them they can be very worthwhile. Typically the US, Germany and the UK are the most lucrative, though only rarely will you get a bigger first advance than you're currently getting in Australia as an established, successful novelist.

Here are the kinds of advances that a successful mid-range author can expect for a first publication offer in another country, per book. Some people will get more, and occasionally a lot more, but don't expect it.

* USD, ** Euros

Some developed countries are difficult to sell to unless you're a major bestselling writer. These include France and Japan. Italy is idiosyncratic – it's difficult to be sure what will sell there.

Royalty rates in most overseas countries tend to be lower than here, e.g. for mass market paperbacks the following are typical for new to mid-range authors (rates may be lower for children's)

Trade paperback and hardcover rates are typically higher:

Don't be surprised if you never see your translated books, or indeed a royalty statement for them. Some small foreign publishers just don't get around to sending them. It's not uncommon for your books to be pirated, especially in Russia, Korea, China, India and various other countries. Do a Google foreign language search on your name and books, and you may be able to discover pirated editions for sale. Whether your agent's foreign agent can do anything about it is another matter, though if your foreign rights are sold by a big multinational publisher they may be able to.

In these countries, even if the advance is paid on time, don't expect to receive any royalties, no matter how well your books sell. You may be lucky, but some foreign publishers simply refuse to pay, or won't acknowledge demands for payment.

*Lesson 48: Sold some foreign rights
and think you've struck it rich?*

There's a widespread misconception that if you've got a British or US deal, you're going to make a fortune because the market is so much bigger. Nothing could be farther from the truth.

These markets are a lot bigger, but they're also savagely competitive and as a foreigner you're at a disadvantage. In your home country you have the edge because you can help promote your books, so your publisher has a stronger incentive to develop your career. In the US and Britain, where the markets are so much bigger, and you're an outsider, there's little you can do on your own even if you frequent the big festivals and conventions, and put up a great web site. Without significant promotion by the publisher, you're unlikely to sell as many copies in either country as you have in your home market.

In the US particularly, unless your book appears in hardcover and/or your publisher brings you over to promote

it, or it has a big promotional push in paperback, it's unlikely to do well. Not impossible – sometimes word-of-mouth will make a book a success without promotion – but pretty unlikely.

And in the US, if you've got three books out and your sales have been poor or declining, you'll probably have to change your name to get any more published. The book buyers don't look any further than the sales trend for your books.

Lesson 49: Movie Rights

It's one of the questions most often asked of writers – when is your book going to be made into a movie? Sadly, for most writers of popular fiction, the answer is never. In any case, you'll rarely sell the movie rights, but rather an option to buy the rights. Movie rights are only bought outright when (a) the producer knows beyond any doubt that the movie is going to be made and has the money and stars lined up, or (b) the writer is a superstar, or (c) the rights can be bought for peanuts. Point (a) takes forever, and point (b) applies to Stephen King, Michael Crichton and their ilk, not you or me.

An option doesn't give the purchaser the film rights, just the option to buy the rights, within a specified period (often a year) for a specified price, or to renew the option once or twice for a similar sum as initially paid. An option ensures that no one else can buy the rights for the period of the option. It is worthless to the buyer unless it specifies the purchase price for the rights, which is why you see in publications that a big name writer has had movie rights to a book optioned for, say, $250,000 versus a $2 million pick-up price. If the movie isn't made the author

keeps the $250,000; if it is, he gets the rest, but not before the first day of shooting.

Many thousands of books are optioned every year, but 98% will never be made into films, because only a few hundred films are made a year and half of those aren't based on existing books anyway. A yearly option typically costs about a tenth of the price of the movie rights. A one-year option for a moderate selling book could be around the $10,000 mark – less if you're a new writer or your sales are very moderate. If you have a modest international bestseller, its movie option could be worth $20-50,000+ per year. In some cases, the option may be renewed for years, a nice little earner even if the movie is never made.

Your book may be based on a great idea, but that doesn't mean the rights will be bought. What matter is sales. Sell 5,000 copies of a book and your idea is worthless – no one's heard of you or it. Sell two million copies and there are two million potential customers for the movie, and that's worth a lot. With such sales you'll certainly sell the movie option for a tidy sum, and there's a good chance it'll get made as well.

Lesson 50: Other subsidiary rights

Check your contract to see which rights you've allowed your publisher to license for you, for how long, what percentage of the income they get for doing so, and which rights you've reserved to yourself. As many as twenty distinct rights could be involved for any book, e.g. serial rights, TV or stage dramatization, merchandising, digest, book club, electronic rights etc, and new ones appear all the time. Most of these will be worth nothing to most authors. Particularly, don't get excited about the recent hype over e-books. Even if you're a mid-range international author, you'll be lucky to make $100 a year from e-book sales.

On the other hand, you never know what rights may become valuable in the future. The estate of TS Eliot is one of the wealthiest of any deceased author; because the musical Cats were based on his 1939 book Old Possum's Book of Practical Cats. And rights that didn't exist when JRR Tolkien signed the contract for The Lord of the Rings have since earned his estate fortunes in royalties. Never give any of your rights away and be suspicious of

anyone who wants them for peanuts – they probably know something you don't.

CHAPTER 6

Lesson 51: Is that all I get?

Shocked that the sales on your royalty statement don't translate into nearly as much money as you expected? Here's what you can actually expect to get, in your hand, for the sale of a single book in various countries. It's calculated on the pre-tax retail price, for typical royalty rates, after your local agent has got her 15% and your overseas agent her percentage. If most of your foreign deals have been done by your publisher, it'll take around 20% agent's fee. Sometimes, e.g. for sales in Eastern Europe or Asia, there could be a local agent involved as well, so after they've all got their share you'll only end up with 50-60% of the advances and the royalties earned.

If you sell enough copies to jump into the higher royalty rate category, you'll get more, of course. The dramatic difference in your share of the overseas mass market editions is due to lower price and/or royalty rates. In Australia you'll generally get 10%, in the UK and US more likely 7.5-8%.

What you get in your hand after agents' cuts, per book

Exch. Rate 0.38, royalty 7.5% to 20K, Aust publisher 20%, Aust agent 15%

Exch. Rate 0.70, royalty 8% to 100K, Aust publisher 20%, Aust agent 15%

Trade paperback and hardcover royalties 10%.

Lesson 52: The Writing business?

Some writers think it's vulgar to go on about money – after all, they write because they love it. That's all very well if you have a job and only write in your spare time, or you're independently wealthy, or have a partner prepared to support you but earning a living as a full-time writer has many challenges. Not at least managing your career so as to maintain that living.

Writers' incomes can fluctuate wildly from one year to the next and, to survive, you need to be professional about every aspect of your career. This means running your writing activities like a business.

All businesses, whether incorporated or not, have costs, and they're considerable. Everything that other people get from their employer (like a furnished office, equipment, travel and promotional expenses, sick leave, superannuation etc) is an expense you have to pay before you earn a cent in salary. Few of these expenses are optional – if you're a registered business you're required by law to have workers comp insurance, to pay superannuation at 9% of total salary, etc. Besides, if you're a full-time

worker you need such things for your own protection. This next Table sets out the range of expenses for a typical writing business. Depending on what you write, some costs may be low, others high, but you can't eliminate them and run a viable business.

Minimum expenses for a viable one-person writing business ($A)

(After agent's fees and GST are paid, i.e. your NET income)

When times are bad, it pays to increase promotion rather than cut it. The same applies when times are good.

* Assumes that you have no borrowings or overdraft. If you do, interest could be thousands more.

** Depends on age/sex/amount of income insured/ smoker etc.

*** Australia , 9% of total salary. Other countries could be more, and may have social security taxes as well.

@ Running costs and servicing only. Assumes car is paid for.

Or more if much overseas travel is involved.

So to run a viable business and pay yourself the moderate salary of $50,000 a year, you must earn minimum of

$80,000 – $100,000 a year from your writing. This may seem like a lot, but no one in any other kind of one-person business, such as your local plumber or computer consultant, or a freelance journalist, could stay in business earning less.

Don't think that kind of income is fantastic and unachievable. Hundreds of Australian writers earn such amounts every year, more than ever before, and thousands of overseas writers. But of course, many writers write full time while earning less, and if you have to write, or while you're building your career and your backlist, pursue the dream no matter what you earn from it.

Lesson 53: Changing publishers

An author's name is like any other brand, and publishers make their money from selling your name as a brand, not a single book. If you're a megastar you may well auction each book to the highest bidder and get away with it. For established mid-range authors, however, changing publishers to get a slightly better deal is gambling with your writing future. You could be better off; alternatively, it may backfire disastrously.

Loyalty cuts both ways and if you leave your publisher without a compelling reason, your old publisher will have little incentive to promote your backlist or contracted books that haven't yet been published. And if your new publisher doesn't promote you effectively, suddenly your career can be on a slide that it's difficult to get off.

But of course, if your publisher is doing nothing for you and you get a great offer from another publisher, the choice is obvious. To establish your name you've got to get a critical mass of sales and readers, so you have to make the most of your opportunities.

Lesson 54: Dealing with Foreign and Local Taxes

There's a whole book in this one. Very briefly, if you're earning money from your books you need to get an ABN and register to pay GST. Your payments from the publisher will include an additional 10% so don't spend it – you've got to pay it with your quarterly return.

Many countries (if not most) have withholding taxes on income you earn there. In some cases, if you go through the agony of discovering what forms have to be filled out, you can get this waived. In others, you just have to lose the money, though generally (where a double taxation agreement exists between that country and Australia) you can claim the tax as a deduction on your Australian tax return. If your foreign sales are made through your Australian publisher you won't have to worry about foreign tax; your publisher will be set up to claim it back, and you should be paid the tax-free amount. Check to make sure that you are.

◆ ◆ ◆

Lesson 55: Anyone who can be discouraged from writing should be

If all this is so disheartening that you plan to give up, you probably weren't meant to be a writer – you just don't want it enough. However, if it's only made you all the more determined, you've got a good chance of making it, for it's the writers who refuse to give up their dream that succeed. I hope you do – the literary world needs more people like you. Just remember that whenever you sit down to write, you're competing with every other writer in the world, in your genre. And when you get there, treat it as a great adventure for as long as it lasts. Don't bet your life on it, for what goes up almost always comes down again. Good luck!

Acknowledgement

Thanks to all the writers and others in the industry that kindly provided comments and information for this book most especially Irvan publishing., and other resourceful books by jerry jerkens and every author out there thank you.